Digging for Indians

Digging for Indians

for Indians

Poems by Gary Gildner

University of Pittsburgh Press

Certain poems in this book (some in slightly different versions) originally appeared in the following magazines: *The Above Ground Review, Colorado State Review, Confluence, Contempora, Crazyhorse, December, Epoch, Field, Foxfire, Hearse, Kansas Quarterly, Laurel Review, Lillabulero, Northwest Review, Poetry Northwest, Quartet, Red Cedar Review, Southern Poetry Review, Sumac, TransPacific, Unicorn Folio, Windsor Review,* and *Voyages.*

"Eeny, Meeny, Miney, Mo, Miss Beech" was first published in *The North American Review.* "The Occupant" is reprinted with permission from *motive* magazine © 1970. "Today Is Sunday" is reprinted with permission of *FOCUS/Midwest* Publishing Company, Inc.

Library of Congress Catalog Card Number 77–158183
ISBN 0–8229–3230–X
ISBN 0–8229–5224–6
Copyright © 1971, Gary Gildner
All rights reserved
Henry M. Snyder & Co, Inc., London
Manufactured in the United States of America

for Judy and Gretchen

What did the Pilgrim Fathers come for, then, when they came so gruesomely over the black sea?

D. H. Lawrence, "The Spirit of Place"

Contents

Part 1   Love Poem   3
P.S.   4
Geisha   5
Harold Fogel Could Be Anywhere   6
Coming Clean   8
Tongues   9
The Visit   10
Midnight Special   11
Today Is Sunday   12
Mark Only One Circle   13
In the Prime Rib   14
Winterset   15
The Crossing   17
Rustling a Hog   18
My Mother Writes . . .   20
Heart Attack   21
Digging for Indians   24

Part 2   Driving to Ankeny   29
Kulick Dreams He's Poet Laureate
   of Little Rhody   31
Not the Pig Farm, but the Poem
   in the Pig Farm   32
Three Chewing Gum Tales   33
Eeny, Meeny, Miney, Mo, Miss Beech   34
A Young Girl's Biology Poem   35
Gathered Around the Chicken Livers   36
I Am a Cossack, Driven by Spring   37
The Day DiMaggio Quit   40
The Occupant   41
"The Classifieds Are Quick"   43
The Haircut   45

Part 3   The Indian Book   49
          The Farm   50
          The Girl in the Red Convertible   53
          Getting Up on Saturday Afternoon in Iowa
              After a Deep Nap and One or Two Memories
              of a Time in Michigan   54
          John & Mary   55
          Why I Quit My Job Digging Bomb Shelters   57
          Don't Worry   58
          Facing the Ladies' Page   59
          Meeting the Reincarnation Analyst   61
          8/22/38—8/22/68   64
          Letter from Des Moines   66
          The Last Monarch of the Season   67

Part

Love Poem

Freckles covered her face and legs.
She kissed—whenever she kissed—the air.
Her blood dried on my lips.
This was in the South in '60.

I was twenty-one and done
with everything; she was seventeen,
a runaway. Our past, which
didn't matter, varied day to day

—or so we told each other
and as fierce as hate believed.
For one whole week inside a room
beside a creek we named "Some Creek

in Tennessee"—we bruised, indifferently.
Then one night it rained; lightning
jumped above the creek and creased
our bellies white. We saw our arms

were crossed and then the same thought
struck us: how our bodies, dead,
would be exposed to all
the gawking rednecks. Turning,

searching in the dark, we dressed
each other's wounds in salt
and lay there, burning,
holding on for love.

P.S.

Tomorrow I will be in Yankton.
South Dakota is the Coyote State.

If you happen to walk
in the park tomorrow
among the cottonwood
and someone is burning leaves
and your hair is still very long and down
and you laugh . . .

The American pasque, the ringnecked pheasant,
        and Pierre
are its flower, bird, and capital.

If you happen to run
through the smoke together
and later drink something hot
and have a fire, an applewood fire
and the air is straight down from Maine
and you are warm all over . . .

On November 2, 1889—exactly eighty years ago
        tomorrow—
it entered the Union.

If you happen to like
his eyes
and lower your own—
I will have already left
for Missoula, followed by Ritzville,
in the Treasure and Evergreen states.

Geisha

The boxer bitch is pregnant
puffed up like an Oriental wrestler!

The boys stand back,
aloof, embarrassed
or unsure of their hands.

But the girls, their cheeks aflame,
are down on shiny knees
praising all the nipples.

The girls of St. Mary's school
were given in puberty
three all-embracing (legal,
religious) rules.

One, do not wear
patent leather shoes.
They reflect
your underwear.

Remember the man
who looked at his face
in the pool too long?
Dead as a cat.

Next, never forget to take
a newspaper
when later
you go on a date.

In case
he should ask you
to sit on his lap—
there is his napkin!

Question? Oh,
you understand;
thank you.
Three, after filling

the tub
sprinkle the surface
with talcum.
This will, believe us,

eliminate visions
when getting in.
Now, one more thing
before you go: God

in all His glory
made the trees—
and they are good
and even necessary.

But from vast
experience we know
that little boys can
shinny up in nothing flat

—especially
when little girls
are walking down below.
So remember, please

keep fast
around the neck,
not to mention
everywhere.

Coming Clean

In the confessional box, erect
waiting my turn to lift my sins
trying not to think of Delphine Bononi's
black impossible cashmere breasts
and my small hands on the velvet
kneeler, I scratch my wrists and sweat

and think, instead, of feeding the ball
to Norm Boyer's belly
of nostrils blowing snot
a clap on the ass in the huddle
of fading back on a perfect fake
and finding my end out, running

waiting, breathing hard
hitting him with the ball, straight
feeling tall as the stands where she sits
her mouth open, red
her knees pink with cold
and of us together

under the covers
among trees
and all summer long
of tasting her tongue with my teeth
of trying to force it, the vision, out, and quit
swallowing spit, the heat

of saying *All over, I kissed her all over*
the silence preceding his words *Impure
Eternal,* the fire
and smell of her skin, of breathing
of closing her eyes, and my own
ripped out, exposed, coming clean, coming clean.

Tongues

Two blondes in bikinis are drinking Schlitz on the grass,
their legs glisten, their eyes say try us.

I stop, having nowhere to go, and lie between them.
They are Charlotte & Charleen, their fathers
are worth a million.

My father is not worth a million.
He was named after the rough Roosevelt
and put to work at ten.

I tell them how Michigan spuds become Michigan lumber,
become Hoover, nickel chickens, Hitler . . .

Nothing rhymes; my guess is
they are bored . . .

After a few years I wake up on my sled—
my father is kicking snow in my face,
he thinks my squealing means *faster!*

Suddenly I pause and insert a parenthesis:
he admired two things mainly—
women and a nail driven straight.
If the first had a workable pretty body
and the second good wood
there was nothing to do but hum.

The girls embrace me for such a warm anecdote.

Wild with emptiness, I stroke their legs.
They burst into several hundred swollen tongues.

The Visit

We embrace & eat
the boiled meat.

Names become sickness,
bad luck, & someone related

is on the verge
of death. In South Dakota

everything is slow.
But

the months pass
along with accidents

& babies. Granny
has her toddy,

falls asleep.
Don't worry—

the bird is fed
& covered—

just worry
about your future.

Now it's time to
catch the News

& Weather.

Midnight Special

Forty-six birds of either sex have enlisted
a topless dancer to flap in their behalf;
no one knows where the birds came from
but the authorities are keeping their eyes peeled.

The dogs of North America are all watching television;
whenever a soap commercial comes on, one gets pregnant;
at last count there were two dozen sheephounds
cleaning their crotches in Washington.

Black-skinned pilot whales, playing follow the leader,
are landing on the beaches of Florida;
real estate dealers from Jacksonville to Miami
are shuffling their feet to beat the band.

Ten Yemenites were publicly beheaded
in the Yemeni capital of San'a;
their bodies were hung
from the chimney with care.

Several English-speaking salvage enthusiasts
have invented a new game called "Body Count";
it will be introduced, God willing,
during the January white sales.

Today Is Sunday

Holding the toast I've spread
with fresh strawberry jelly,
I read where the Reverend
Marvin Proctor says the war
"is partly a war against
heathen religions." It would be
wrong to stop. Elsewhere,
scientists say it won't be long
before we can kiss off
Lake Michigan. Sore spots
on the local front: white firemen
are not speaking to the de-
partment's only black; blight
is winning over trees; four teens
burn two cats "because we wanted to
hear them scream"; a bat attacks
a lady while she sleeps, but
an official smashes the bat's brains
with an empty Pepsi bottle. And Iowa's morals,
according to a Mason City man,
are going straight
to hell. I pause
to take my first bite.
The toast is cold, and hateful.

Mark Only One Circle

Mark only one circle.
Mark "hot water" even if you have it only part time.
Are you white, black, Japanese, or Other?
If you are "Other" print race.
If you are Indian print tribe.
Erase mistakes completely.

Have you ever been knocked out?
How long were you unconscious?
Did it hurt?
Did it hurt very much, not very much, none of these?
Does anyone outside the immediate family use your "facilities"?

If you went down for the count, did your mouth volunteer
    tiny bubbles?
Did anyone giggle?
Did a lady in a sporelike lavender hat
    or an ape in red suspenders kick
    a midget popcorn vendor full
    speed on the knee
    because they couldn't see around him?

Have you ever wanted to drown your sorrows?
Are you sick and tired of being out of shape?
Are you sick and tired of dropping your guard?
If elected, will you promise not to come back?

In the Prime Rib

I was in the Prime Rib, trying to stay dry,
when I learned from the guy on my left
that the going rate for blowing off a kneecap
in the hick state of Iowa
was one hundred dollars
—"if," he said, squeezing his olive,
"you know the right people."

I turned to my right, and a lady
sucking her Bloody Mary through a straw
took my hand. Harry, she said,
had taken to painting naked women
by filling in the numbered areas
—did I know what it was doing?
—did I know it was driving her up the wall?

Then they both started chewing
their ice cubes in my ears,
and they kept at it until the barman appeared,
to wonder what I was trying to pull.
"Nothing," I said, and pulled on my gloves.
Outside, people were still rushing each other,
still splashing blood, and cursing animals.

There's an Irish graveyard on a hill near Winterset
  and there are dates that tell of famine & escape
  and there's a church, a hornet stuck in wax
  and down below the lowest grave a stream
    that huddles in the mud

And there are covered bridges made of cedar in the area
  some are leaning awkwardly like bloated birds
  some are straight & painted red against the weather

And in the town itself a grassy Square
  boys in Fords are cruising with their collars up
  men in overalls are sitting down around the Square
    & looking at their shoes

And at the Nixon Feed the sun is lighting up a fly
  that's dying in the window by an axe

And in the bakery a purple cake goes round & round
  & wishes "68" good luck

And at the Standard someone's radiator's hot
  & blowing steam, & someone yells
    "Don't touch it!"

A Frankenstein is showing at the Iowa

In the corner barbershop the blinds are drawn
  a shadow moves behind the glass
  a Ford purrs by out front, & then another
  color photos in the door declare John Wayne
    a local son
  declare the house where he was raised
  declare his horse & guns
  declare his fist & face
  declare his race
  declare the way in Winterset

The Crossing

We are in our tenth month of crossing.
It is so hot, touch is impossible.
This morning we killed Park, the medical student;
his red tongue burst,
his gritty blood did not go far enough.

We hate to begin on the animals
—as bitter as it is, their urine
holds back bickering and random stabbings.
But our mouths cry
for water,

and we are seeing things nightly we had not dreamed—
great raw crows
brush our faces and leave
a sweet, meaty odor in their wake.
Everyone has boils

and sleeps with his knife.
No one disliked Park;
he was small, and drank from his wrists
rather than bend behind the animals.
He would die anyway.

Rustling a Hog

1

Arrive
at night.
Bring beer in case
you have to wait
—some son of a bitch might
be outside leaking, screwing
off or something.

Speak
in pig-talk.
Don't leave clues, like wing
your cans around.
Also, winter's bad—
snow & polka dots.
Pull it off in fall.

Choose a juicy
young one. Ordinarily a ball-
peen hammer *wap!*
between the eyes
(that soft spot there)
will do the job.
Then blow.

2

Clean & bleed it.
Dig a pit & fire charcoal.
Man, don't forget

the bastard's wormy—
turn him
till he's crisp.

By the fire
drop, from time to time, a gob of spit
& tell your story.

Watch your girl
feel her jeans & wiggle.
Cut the sweetmeat loose,

trim it.
Notice how your spaniel flops
& laps her crotch.

She's nervous. After eating
suck your fingers,
check around. Pick your teeth.

My Mother Writes . . .

My mother writes to wonder
why I missed Christmas
on top of Thanksgiving—
she brought a turkey up

from the freezer
baked a juicy ham
and, if I can imagine, peeled
sweet potatoes, onions, luscious Idahoes

and beets beets beets until
my father asked, "Are you crazy?"
No, but someday

the blood will squirt
from her head and face
because the pills she takes for the zooming pressure
are breaking her heart

and nothing tastes like it used to
if I can imagine.

Heart Attack

The day
my father's heart attacked
and knocked him down
in Michigan,

I was pulling huskies
off a woodchuck
in a thicket up in Canada—
he'd turned to make a stand,

having lost his balance.
There was nothing left
except the claws,
a rag of fur,

and blood,
like makeup,
on the lead dog's smiling
stuffed-toy face.

Later,
when I got the call
from home,
they told me not to worry—

he was plugged in
to the best machine, and a nurse's eyes
were on him
day and night.

I downed
two shots of bourbon, felt
my chest contract,
and then

at fifteen thousand feet
I watched a blonde
with fuzz above her lip
pass out pin-on wings

to balding lovers
buckled in the belly.
Then I slept,
dreaming that we touched

down in Flint,
where I found him
wired
to a television set.

The doctor said,
"We call this level line his heart."
I was afraid
to shake his hand,

the hand
that showed me how to hold
a hammer,
and sat down;

his nails,
shiny as a baby's,
lay between us.
Overhead, the chalkline hummed

in blue.
Fifteen minutes passed.
I tried to kiss him
but I couldn't move my lips.

"Remember the day
I kicked snow in your face?
How you squealed!
And I kept thinking you meant

go faster—faster—"
The nurse reared up
—"Go easy"—
then sat back

and rolled her eyes,
as if she'd heard that story too!
He lowered his voice—a good boy—
and whispered

he couldn't stand
or breathe without feeling
the ice
coming up in his lungs—

and falling,
falling into head-high drifts
he wished
for something warm to wear—

and grabbed
my hunting shirt.
I woke,
we were on the ground.

A girl's hand
was pinned against my chest,
and she was crying, "Please,
oh please let go—"

Digging for Indians

The first week the soil was clean,
except for a shrew's lobster-
colored jaw, a bull snake caught
in its long final bellow,
and an ocher mouse holding
its head, as if our trowels had given it
a migraine. Then we hit bird-bone
beads, clam shells,

and then we struck a spine.
Digging slowly we followed it
north, toward a stand of cottonwood
overlooking the river and, beyond,
a patch of abandoned pickups and plows
taking the sun.
We stopped
below the shoulder blades for lunch.

Then we resumed, working down
and into the body,
now paring
the dirt like exotic fruit,
now picking between the ribs
as if they were bad teeth
aching with impacted meat.
We were dripping wet,

and slapping at sweat bees
attacking the salt
on our backs—
but he was taking shape,
he was beginning to look,
as his pelvis came through,
like a man. We uncovered
his thighs and brittle, tapering feet,

and then we went for his skull.
Shaving close, slicing off
worms that curlicued
like brains out of place,
we unearthed his hollow expression,
his bony brow,
and finally, in back of his neck,
an arrowhead stuck to the vertebrae.

The ground rumbled under our knees—
Quickly we got the Polaroid
and snapped him from several angles—
except for the scattered fingers
we could not have planned a better specimen . . .
Then we wrapped him up in foil.
Tomorrow we would make a plaster cast,
and hang it in the junior college.

Part 2

Driving to Ankeny

She was naked—straight ahead
and smack between the cornstalks
closing in. So I slowed down,
reached over, and stroked her
on the knee—exactly where
the sun had touched it rouge!
Warmed up, I had to stop
and then my nerve expanded
quietly and quietly I found her fur.
You know how a trout will hold
so still, just before you dip

your finger in the pool? Her eyes—
I mean they didn't move, and yet
they had killdeer braking down
for miles around, screaming
I am here   I am here
and there I was! All skin & bones
and on the verge of everything if
only she would move
or make a sound. *Love*,
I said, *we know each other. Look!*
I am here   here

It didn't work. In fact her face
just lay there like the land's.
Well, there was nowhere else to go
but Ankeny and so
I shifted into first
and drove that way. Oh now and then
you turn and catch a cow
in pure relief, a sow
scratching her belly . . .
But it's not enough
to keep you from dreaming.

Kulick Dreams He's Poet Laureate
of Little Rhody

A white-haired gentleman in red socks
& gold on most of his bottom
teeth, he laughs on time to Mrs. Ida Grove's good
bustline, & starts to sip his tea—

No!—& she
grabs him by the neck &
wrings &
things get sweaty—

Out of his mouth flies
a peony, a crow, & his feet, a couple
of cocky volunteers, begin
to badger the throw rug—

Aha! Old K. knows a joke
when he sees one, slaps his thigh *kerr-ack!*
confesses a liking for Roger (The Fingers) Williams
—& leaps for the door

where Ida, Miss Providence of 1937, shoves
a buck in his violet
& in front of frankly a million customers
pets the state chicken to death.

Not the Pig Farm,
but the Poem in the Pig Farm

1

Coagulum cacciatore.
Wallace! there's a poem
in this. Look how those mothers,
simply by nosing the dirt—
look how they circulate
so much tit.

2

They are not chintzy
or immoral—
nor Scottish crocks
and footballs.
"They are round"
and get around, eventually.

3

And the piggies!
One has the scours
and runs in a corner,
another bumps its ruptured
navel on the ground, going off
toward the water trough.
But the others on their nipples
kick and wiggle, suck
and fill. It's "the way
they are modelled"—blind
to the observer, overwhelmed.

Three Chewing Gum Tales

1

Eleven sparrows are pecking on the roof
of the auditorium. But their pecking is pointless,
there is not a seed, not a dried-up fly
to be found anywhere. Suddenly
a twelfth sparrow lands, and brings with him
twelve sticks of chewing gum.

2

There is a girl called The Golden Girl.
There is a boy called The Boy from Bloomington.
They insist they have everything in common.
They admit that "everything in common"
is probably just an expression.
Nonetheless, they insist upon it, their mouths
in almost perfect harmony,
until one and then the other goes to sleep.

3

Time is running out on old "39."
We see him wearing a dog's head.
We see him watching a coed's neck being nuzzled into.
We see him exposing his yellow socks while cheering
for a "split up the middle!"
After the snap and the weeping and laughing
we no longer see him.
There is only a vague echo, a chill,
and chewing gum wrappers.

Eeny, Meeny, Miney, Mo, Miss Beech

I loved Miss Beech
my kindergarten teacher
hard enough to give up spitting
in the fishbowl,
hard enough to lick
her yellow hair in dreams
for years. She told us doves
were gentle, wolves
were mean. I believed
everything she whispered.
Then one day I saw
the raw body of a dove
its mate, in heat, had flayed alive.
I hunted down a book
and read that fighting wolves
have something in their blood
to cool it,
even when the weaker gives
its vein.
Oh Miss Beech, that night
I offered you my bone.
You took it in your hands
and broke it.

A Young Girl's Biology Poem

Yesterday it was a grasshopper
three pairs of legs millions of eggs
and the male actually gets on top

Today the dogfish shark
the girl's sort of odd because she grows
her young inside but doesn't nurse it
and the old man dogfish gets his business done
conducting through a fin

Tomorrow it's a cat
and no one's looking forward to it
they're expensive they're embalmed
just like a person

I wish we'd stick to movies
earlier we saw the starfish
funny starfish only spray
their fish-producing parts into the water
they're not even fish they're echinoderms poor things
they force their stomachs in a clam
and suck it clean

Gathered around the chicken livers
they are discussing cameras
in glass penises.
This device appears, says one, to represent a breakthrough,
or contributes rather to a breakdown
of certain myths; to wit, the female
does not lubricate
willy-nilly,
and wipes his chin.

After him a lady passing carrot sticks
chips in her Seminar on Sex
and the eye-opening movies
she'd been ex-
posed to
in the cellar of the Wesley House.
There were none of your Elks or Moose
or any of those people smoking like crazy,
she wants to make plain;
this was educational,
especially "The Coed"—formerly called "The Nun"—
just to menton one
that demonstrated everything.

What, the host wonders, filling the candy dish,
happened exactly?
Oh, you had to be
there in the flesh, she says,
to feel your hang-ups
practically evaporate!
—and to see how really beautiful
it was, all those wives and husbands, watching,
fourteen hours straight, together!

I Am a Cossack, Driven by Spring

1

Last night we squealed off
in Tiger Bradshaw's fluid drive '49 Buick, swigging
from bottles of bourbon-spiked
Pepsi-Cola and
talking up visions of Gypsies
in silver underpants,
for The Flame.

2

Before the girls came on, a man in fish-
belly cheeks
and his left ear missing
("for heroics," he bug-eyed, "in Rome")
introduced a juicy
and ED-you-
cational strip
of celluloid entitled
"Ten Days in Nature"—

       All

we saw
were naked ladies playing
volleyball, and
shaking a lot
in a shaky brown tint
—while an underwater voice explained
that girls in India
covered their faces, whereas
Western women hid
their "coveted
public places."

3

Then Sister Mack said *Lad*
you have knucklebones
on the brain
—and rapped my skull.
In return
I pounced on her slowball,
rocked it
back through the box,
and broke her beak.

4

Then Tiger, that son of a bitch,
said *Who's up next?*
It was Florida's own
Faye LaFay, who dropped
her negligee and let
the drummer brush her
creamy butt.

5

Boys in every box of candy
a hitherto unreleased
and unretouched photy graph
of Maxine
facing the camera

But it was Peaches Parker
from Charlottesville, who rode her
long red hair cowboy style, while bouncing
two freckled melons

on some old gentleman's
sweaty head.
It was Uncle Andy from Cincinnati
up from the front row,

and I was in Detroit, at The Flame,
alone,
standing before the warped, obscenely
penciled plywood
blocking the doors,

knocking,
and no one
would let me in.

6

I walked home over knucklebones and dog crap.
Once, trying for six feet,
I slipped in the grass.
A sympathetic cat nudged my cheek.
I offered her a drink—
she pulled her tail through the hedge
and disappeared.

7

This morning,
my Lithuanian neighbor is quietly mending
his fence. He is using screws; he knows
I broke it last night, mad
to spy his Velma's bed dance
and smoke.

The Day DiMaggio Quit

The day DiMaggio quit
I was rubbing oil
on your back, feeling

your skin so cool
under that white sun
I could not believe

I was touching,
love. You were
brushing off

your knees, watching
two gulls dive
and split

the spray. Hot
and young. That's how
I remembered it.

The Occupant

He keeps camouflaging his house
with fallen walnut twigs
and angry letters to the Interior . . .

Because there is a target in his rec room,
a riddled target embedded in cement block,
that someone tried to hide behind the juke box.

Because his daughter, in long black panty hose,
is meeting her philosophy teacher
behind the band shell these nights
and bothers to keep him posted.

Because tied to the juke box is a tag which yells
DO NOT MOVE.
He likes to move.
He likes to know what's going on.
He can remember slipping in his nickels
and dancing to "In the Mood."

Because his wife is at Newcomers, Books,
Cancer, Heart Disease, or Antiques,
but he can't be sure
—he lost her itinerary.

Because why would anyone move the juke box
to hide a target?

Because he took a knife to the blocks
and couldn't pick out the bullets
—they were too far in.

Because his mother writes: "When we die
our bodies will scream"—
and adds to that love, season's greetings,
and a postscript he can't understand.

Because he rubbed putty in the holes
and put on several coats of white,
and felt better because the rec room looked nicer
and everything stood out much clearer . . .
but only for a moment.

Because the postscript finally unfolds, to declare:
his father's place at the table
has been replaced by chrome legs
and a row of identical hard green flowers.

Because he often thinks he is the only one
who doesn't know the joke . . .
and because he keeps piling twigs
around his windows and doors,
and writing letters that come back: ADDRESSEE UNKNOWN.

"The Classifieds Are Quick"

In hot, cold, or indifferent seasons
he is always wanted
by someone, somewhere . . .

Aggressive? Ambitious? Burning
to make it Big!
Yes. Oh yes!

Well then,
"Recognition Becomes You!"
—and his head swims
in possibilities his eyes
can't follow fast enough—

For he, too, can operate a clamshell crane.
Drive a Thunderbird from coast to coast.
Guard, from midnight until morning breaks
innocent around their limbs,
the student nurses in their Lutheran parking lot.
Or learn, in forty weeks, karate.

Yes! He can stay in touch with fun!
Can kiss the lonely, bored, discouraged, *common*
life good-by and mix
three nights a week with others over 30, under 55.
Can send his résumé to Mr. Short, Box 48,
who has the product,
prospects, high commissions,
unabused expense accounts, Blue Cross!
—in fine, everything but Tigers
he can train to get a signature
and close a deal.

Yes. But he must not sit back, bite his nails
and wish, "If only I had Spanish *and* phys. ed.
I could teach in Pleasant Valley—"

No. Nor say, again, "Oh yes,
my home is good—"
and settle for the free, litter-
trained part-Persian . . .

And the next day wring his hands
and advertise the one he has.

The Haircut

After several butchered trims
from nurses in intensive care
my father, shaggy as a sheep dog,
goes to Lem the barber.
Lem sells bows and arrows, reloads spent
shotgun shells and sharpens knives
on the side. On the walls, on the mirror,
everywhere the same flushed face
is grinning down between the horns
of mountain goats, over water buffalo,
beside a line of deer hung up to dry.

My father takes the chair
while Lem goes in the woods
with slugs . . .
"That sucker fooled me once . . .
But when he stuck his antlers in my hairs . . ."
I watch
my father in the glass—a row
of Lucky Tiger lotion cuts his back in half . . .

Lem tags his kill
then whistles, pointing scissors
at a miniskirted girl outside.
She swings away as Lem attacks
my father's locks. "Hey where's
the old man been," he winks at me,
"out spotting beaver . . .?"

Laughter from the next in line—

"Goddam!" Lem says and pulls

a clipping from his shirt. "You read about
this husky dog the Japs
all aim to stuff and stick
in some museum?
Can't say the breed—
but anyway . . ." and Lem reports

in 1958 the Japanese
in the Antarctic
left their sled dogs wrapped in chains;
back in '59 they found
a couple loose, alive.
One soon died but Taro, welcomed home a hero,
lived to be fifteen.

Chin down, Lem fights his gas—
"Beats the shit
out of me how he lived"—
then burps it up.
His clippers finish off
my father's neck; a razor
goes around the lowered ears.
"The main thing is don't freeze
between the legs"—
                          and Lem is through.
He whips away the sheet.
My father pays. Going out
we hear the barber stomp his foot, and whoop—
"Hot damn! I wished I had a husky dog like that. Don't you?"

Part

For tradition
they put in potbellied Paiutes trying their luck
in Pyramid Lake, Nevada, which is drying up.

For loss of tradition and desperation
they put in latter-day Six Nation Iroquois sporting
warbonnets never worn by Six Nation Iroquois.

For color
they put in a Sioux skewered—like fresh kabob—to a stick,
while spectators wait for his skin to rip.

For color and madness
they put in Satanta, big-jawed, tight-eyed
and troublesome, who when captured committed suicide.

For domesticity, just in case,
they put in squaws chewing the fat, Shoshone
style, beside a cyclone fence in outer Wyoming.

For the record
they put in Geronimo, Chief Joseph—all those grim
rebels who finally got sense and cashed in.

For pathos, guilt, etc.
they put in a King Island Eskimo kid
in front of shacks and TV antennas bent by the wind.

The Farm

I watch the old barn lean
and think: *the swallows will hold it up*
and in an emergency run
screaming for help
then turn toward the creek
the Prince Albert can on my hip.
I'd found it, faded to a light rosé,
in a heap of harnesses and junk.
Once, we'd fill these bright
red cans with crawlers
and a chunk of dirt for perch
and bass and pike.
Never suckers: those we took
the hayforks after, working
squeeze plays on them
at the wide, pebbly turn
where the creek goes shallow—
and freeze our feet and shins
by staying in too long
but hardly wince, flipping
sucker after sucker up the bank
and fiercely keeping score.
Later, kneeling in the sun
we'd slice their bellies
and, good surgeons, slip

the long flat tapeworms out.
We tossed the worms at trees
or draped them over posts
to treat the crows,
as up the hill we hauled our catch
going past the wet-nosed bull
whose cock our cousin showed us
was a slim pink sword
by offering the bull a milker's
bony haunch (our city eyes bugged out
but she just chewed her cud and drooled)—
and at the pigpen
handed in our kill, quick
to keep our fingers from the old sow's snout.
Then we hit the fields for fat
tomatoes, cucumbers and radishes
—and down the hill again
to wash them in the creek, chasing
with our cuke torpedoes
schools of minnows—
and remember suddenly
to check between our toes
for oily bloodsuckers;
always finding some, we'd scrape
them off with sand (and pray

that none had crawled
in our ears
or up our butts when swimming.)
On the bridge we sprawled
across the logs and ate, reciting
batting averages; the truly great
were always dead—except for
maybe Williams and DiMaggio . . .
and getting up we'd sprint
toward the woods, where uncles
flashing lights last fall
froze deer before the season,
and over whiskey and smoked sturgeon bragged
how sweet the corn-fed bucks
whose pricks were never used,—
then stopping, taking off our shirts, a leaf
of wintergreen between our teeth,
we'd lie on moss
or soft pine needles, lazily
bring down a hawk
with sticks of birch that served as 30-30's,
or just peel them,
and slowly start to dream
of sending daring messages,
written on the stiff clean bark.

The Girl in the Red Convertible

The girl in the red convertible
with the heater going full blast
and her throat knocking
turns off the lights
on the road to Winterset
and rolls toward the moon
resting expressionless
on the next hill.

When the car stops coasting
it is still June, and
she is at the edge
of a field, waiting . . .
She has a
"fifty-fifty chance." It—
that expression—is quietly
eating her eyeballs . . .

At dawn a cow appears; then
another. Taking all the time
they need. If only something
would break—break open
so she could scream—
Finally there are nine lined up
along the fence—
like visitors to the zoo.

Getting Up on Saturday Afternoon in Iowa After a Deep Nap and One or Two Memories of a Time in Michigan

I am thinking of the green-eyed girl who loved
a trumpet player once and how
when his throat got sweaty and his veins
were big and blue and almost bursting
she could close her eyes and never need
to see again, and how we walked
all one Sunday on the apple farm
her father talked of taking on in Orchard Lake
near Pontiac before he ran away
and how the man who had it then surprised us, shouting
"Who the hell are you!" and how
one Saturday she came in, out of breath,
and kissed me in the tub and warmed her fingers
on my cheeks and shared her carrot
that she lifted from the Grosse Pointe A & P
and how we crashed the Catholic church
on Woodward Avenue one Monday night and lit
a candle for his hair and eyes and hoped
he didn't suffer much the night they slit
his happy throat and left him in Grand Circus Park
to watch the sun come up in Canada and die.

John & Mary

John says all the girls
go nuts when he's around
—except his sisters who
pound his head off and are ugly.

Mary shakes her braids; explains
he's on his back, he's
an *accident*
with bones poking in the grass.

John jumps up and scratches—
no, he's in the Army,
cocks his hands
and shouts *OK you Commie bastards!*

Mary, shrieking, runs
behind a tree; John drops
to one ripped knee
—his eyes are peeled.

Suddenly a sniper starts to fire.
The girl appears: John,
I've got my heels on,
let's pretend we're married.

He shakes his head: he can't,
he's bleeding bad. He
grabs a stick
and hits the dirt.

But you can be
the dad, she says, and
drive the car—or
just be happy fixing houses.

Come on, John,
let's pretend we're friends.
No, he says, and rolling over
Tommy guns the sparrows.

Why I Quit My Job Digging Bomb Shelters

Because it was hot
dusty my feet burned my eyes burned
my ears hurt the rig belching oil
smelled the customers

Because you turned simply
and looked
taking me in my skin breathing
I wanted to dive
be a frog
cool on your knees

Because the worms were shouting
angry disrupted complaining afraid

Because your lips were on the verge

and laughing delirious
I wanted to splash hear birds applaud
feel the wind lie down
the fish go straight
and the grass around us explode

Don't Worry

if California oozes
up through two states
& a piece of Oklahoma
into Wichita,

if the Kansas drama
lady grabs your head
to understand why
they are running naked

in New York, & cheese
Mustangs are raising
a stink in Sweetwater
—don't worry.

You've got your feet
propped up, mother
robin is feeding
her monsters,—

& as long as the worms
don't disappear
we're safe.

Facing the Ladies' Page

I was flat on my back on the morning paper—
the day was so fresh
I couldn't resist lying down in it.
Then I rolled over, into a nose job . . .

A bobbed proboscis may tend
to emphasize a double chin—but no sweat,
you can chop one off.

And if your breasts are flabby
or your head is shedding its only coat,
why be a shrinking violet?—
plastic surgery will slim you down,
sprout you out!

All I wanted to do was take a nap—
now I'm thinking maybe soon
I'll need a follicle
or, even worse,
a testicle transplant . . .

This is a feature article!
and I'm afraid to turn the page.

"Irate Mother" tells Ann Landers
her nervous son Yule had to share
his hospital room with a man about seventy,
a cardiac failure who looked almost dead.
Two days after Yule's minor surgery
his roommate died, and Yule's recovery
was slowed by a week. Mother wonders,
"Is there anyone we can sue?"

This is a cartoon, I'm in stitches,
but why am I laughing—I'm not insured!

"No Longer Frightened" writes in:
"I was frightened batty
when I had my first baby,
not of childbirth but of holding him."
One day a neighbor explained, "If you worry,
you don't trust; if you trust, you don't worry."
Ann answers, "How beautiful! Thank you."

So don't get screwed up: if you suffer
from blotchy birthmarks, take injections
of a white compound under the skin,—
it's much like tattooing.
This is trustworthy, easy, antiseptic,
therapeutic, beautiful, patriotic, a poem!

A poem that smells,
dreams,
walks, talks,
believes,
and even lets a little water
out the proper hole.

And if you pinch it
it will cry.

Meeting the Reincarnation Analyst

I guess because it was Key West
and I was a little drunk
I expected some ridiculous facsimile
of Sidney Greenstreet, puffing hard, to slip
through the beaded curtains first—
to set me up with secrets smirking
on his sweaty mug.

But nobody like that came in
to the Immortality Consultation Room
off Whitehead Street that smelled
of incense, salt, and cat shit—
just Patricia Peel, Ph.D.,
the mystic in a flaming beehive
hairdo, teardrop earrings, and a sheet.

She offered me her hand—snakes and snappers,
swordfish, flies and eyeballs
—these were on the rings
her fingers wiggled at me.
On the middle knuckle of her middle
finger, dominating all the fauna,
was a baby's skull, in gold.
I kissed her blue-veined wrist.

She said, "Please sit"—
and pointed to the satin sofa.
At my side she opened up her sheet
to show a copper cross inlaid
with writhing octopuses
hanging down between her breasts.
"You have," she said, "six former lives
and many, many Karmic ties—"

I interrupted: "Have you really got a Ph.D.?"
She continued, "—and in each past life
you loved an evil woman."
The first, reported Dr. Peel, was a Carib maiden
taken by Cortez to entertain him
on the voyage back to Spain . . .
"She succumbed to lust, disease, and worms."

My mystic gripped her cross.
"The second girl, a Salem witch,
 accused of lying down with pigs—"
"Hey wait a minute," I said.
But Dr. Peel spoke on, her eyes
as hard and green as early walnuts,
killing off my Salem witch by stuffing
down her throat her lovers' testicles.

An octoroon of Jefferson's
who later slept with Madison,
and a Cajun who was burned
alive with John Wilkes Booth
were my ladies three and four
and I had had it. I dropped
the Consultation fee in Patty's lap, and left.

That night, in my air-conditioned Holiday,
I showered with a smiling bonefish—
then fixed a gin and tonic,
and watched debilitated Ponce de León
arrive in Florida at Eastertide
above my bed. Oh, I'd love to say
she came around without her junk,
and that we had a laugh, and maybe
even said what we were looking for.
But the truth is no one came,
and the next day I moved on.

What did you do last summer?
Last summer I turned the corner.

What did you think about?
Tad Weed—who weighed 116 pounds and booted
goals for Ohio State.

Did you ever try anything foolish?
Once I tried a drop-kick and missed.

Were you a hit in high school?
The coach flinched and called me a fool.

What did you do on your birthday?
Kept in touch.

What else?
Sold my Austin-Healey, felt sorry.

What else?
Practiced my craft, ground my teeth.

What else?
Missed my calling.

What else?
Ate hard-boiled eggs with angry horseradish,
feisty leeks and cold sliced tomatoes.

How did you feel?
Ready.

What for?
Albacore tuna and tender green peas
in a butter and onion and pepper white sauce.

Then what?
The sun settled down behind Audubon, Iowa.

How did you feel?
No bigger than a minute.

Letter from Des Moines

Dear B.— I miss the mountains.
Yesterday, riding my bike in the rain,
I almost hit a bluejay
just standing in Brattleboro Street;
a soggy cigarette butt
was stuck in its beak.

On the plane back I sat between
a man who manufactures artificial limbs, "really slick"
tubs for cripples, and a girl who swallows
swords in California.
He slipped her his
"Missouri Valley Brace Co." card;
she wrote her number down in lipstick.

I am restless. I miss the clean dives
of frogs, the nibbled witch hobble.
My students, most of them, are calm.
They dream, to the rim of their teeth,
of going Greek.
The carefully nervous few
have signalled me to choose up sides.

When the weather's nice
I pull up weeds
(the fat grubs had a good summer)—
when it's not, I ride to the park
and watch the deer bed down,
and think how warm their bellies are,
and how long winter will be.

The Last Monarch of the Season

When I come back
with it in my hands

careful not to bruise the color
of its life

release it to the pillow, say
that I have touched

its trembling only—

When I come back
and lay my lips

uncovered
near its wings

and put your fingers
over them forever

once again—

When I do all of this
in prelude to your kiss

will you let me go
in the morning?

PITT POETRY SERIES

James Den Boer, *Learning the Way*
 (1967 U.S. Award of the International Poetry Forum)
James Den Boer, *Trying to Come Apart*
Jon Anderson, *Looking for Jonathan*
Jon Anderson, *Death & Friends*
John Engels, *The Homer Mitchell Place*
Samuel Hazo, *Blood Rights*
David P. Young, *Sweating Out the Winter*
 (1968 U.S. Award of the International Poetry Forum)
Fazıl Hüsnü Dağlarca, *Selected Poems*
 (Turkish Award of the International Poetry Forum)
Jack Anderson, *The Invention of New Jersey*
Gary Gildner, *First Practice*
Gary Gildner, *Digging for Indians*
David Steingass, *Body Compass*
Shirley Kaufman, *The Floor Keeps Turning*
 (1969 U.S. Award of the International Poetry Forum)
Michael S. Harper, *Dear John, Dear Coltrane*
Ed Roberson, *When Thy King Is A Boy*
Gerald W. Barrax, *Another Kind of Rain*
Abbie Huston Evans, *Collected Poems*
Richard Shelton, *The Tattooed Desert*
 (1970 U.S. Award of the International Poetry Forum)
Adonis, *The Blood of Adonis*
 (Syria-Lebanon Award of the International Poetry Forum)
Norman Dubie, *Alehouse Sonnets*